Star in my Forehead

Star in my Forehead

SELECTED POEMS BY
ELSE LASKER-SCHÜLER

TRANSLATED BY
JANINE CANAN

HOLY COW! PRESS · DULUTH, MINNESOTA · 2000

The translator thanks the editors of *Aporia, California Quarterly, Caprice,
Carbuncle, Cybercorpse.org, European Judaism, Israel Horizons, Isthmus, Mosaic,
Multiples* and *Tree,* who published some of these poems in earlier translations.

She also thanks Kösel Verlag for permission to publish translations of poems
from *Sämtliche Gedichte* by Else Lasker-Schüler (Munich, 1966).

Illustrations are from *Sämtliche Gedichte* by Else Lasker-Schüler, and *Franz
Marc, Postcards to Prince Jussuf* by Peter-Klaus Schuster (Prestel Verlag,
Munich, 1988). All drawings, except those by Karl Schmidt-Rottluff and
Franz Marc, are by Else Lasker-Schüler.

Library of Congress Cataloging-in-Publication Data

Lasker-Schüler, Else, 1869-1945.
(Poems, English & German. Selections)
Star in my forehead: selected poems / Else Lasker Schueler;
translated by Janine Canan.
p. cm.
English and German.
ISBN 0-930100-88-3 (pbk.)
1. Lasker-Schèler, Else, 1869-1945—Translations in English.
I. Canan, Janine. II. title.
PT2623.A76 A23 2000
831'.912—dc21   99-87465

Holy Cow! Press books are distributed to the trade by Consortium Book
Sales & Distribution, 1045 Westgate Drive, Saint Paul, Minnesota 55114.
Our books are available through all major library distributors and jobbers,
and through most small press distributors, including Bookpeople and Small
Press Distribution. For personal orders, catalogs or other information, write
to: Holy Cow! Press
Post Office Box 3170
Mount Royal Station
Duluth, Minnesota 55803

To the Shekinah

Contents

III. OUR LOVE SONG (1913-1923)

IV. MY BLUE PIANO (1932-1945)

PREFACE

I FIRST BECAME AWARE OF JANINE CANAN'S revelatory translation of Lasker-Schüler's poetry in 1970, when she offered a group to an issue of *Tree* whose thematic focus was Shekinah, the exiled female reality of the Divine. Up to that point, my perception of Lasker-Schüler was the standard-issue image of an exotic Viennese eccentric, as H.D. or Mina Loy were often perceived, objects of reverential neglect. Lasker-Schüler's minimal presence in English-language literature consisted of a few sentimental translations from *Hebraische Balladen*.

In this comprehensive gathering, Janine Canan directs our attention to Lasker-Schüler's writing, returning us to the ground of the poem, and away from often negative obstacles of literary mythology. Canan offers a rare and unexpected blessing of a poet who shares a deep affinity for another poet, and is able to translate her work from one language into another without erasing those essences structuring the original texts.

It is hoped that this volume will serve as prelude to equally sympathetic translations of Lasker-Schüler's other writings, her memoirs, essays, and the play *Arthur Anonymous*. But, for now, we must remain unremitting in our gratitude for what Janine Canan has accomplished.

—*David Meltzer*

TRANSLATOR'S NOTE

BORN IN THE RHINELAND IN 1869, Else Lasker-Schüler migrated to Berlin in her youth, consorted with Expressionists in the first decades of the century, published ten books of poetry and prose, and in 1932, age sixty-three, received Germany's prestigious Kleist Prize. Months later "the greatest lyric poet of modern Germany," as she was considered by many, was accosted by Nazis waving an iron bar. The poet ran straight to the train station, took the next train to Zurich, and never returned to Germany. From Switzerland she voyaged to Palestine, where she died twelve years later, at the age of seventy-six.

Else Lasker-Schüler was buried on the Mount of Olives with a tombstone from the Sea of Galilee. I was three years old at the time, living with my family in Los Angeles. When I was a small child, my mother often sang to my sister and me; later when in my teens Mother began studying German—in order to sing the beautiful songs of Schumann, Schubert and Brahms—I joined her. The next year I entered Stanford University, and continued with German. I longed to read the German poets, above all Rilke. At twenty, I graduated from Stanford and entered the German department at the University of California in Berkeley, where I studied for three years. There I was introduced to Else Lasker-Schüler in a course taught by Professor Heinz Politzer, who had known the sibyl-poet during her last years in Palestine.

In 1966, while living in Berlin, I came upon *Else Lasker-Schüler: Sämtliche Gedichte*, an illustrated red volume, newly released by Kösel Verlag in celebration of the centenary of the poet's birth. Perhaps some similarity between Else's mystical temperament and my own, or the Jewish piece in my maternal background, or some other karmic connection magnetized me to her work. Right away I began translating her poems. And I continued to do so for the next three decades, as I became a psychiatrist, wrote and published poetry of my own. Kaleido-scopically shifting over the years, like flowers unfolding, my translations were endlessly revised. In the early years they were scrupulously literal. Later on, as my relationship to the poet deepened and I traveled further into her visionary landscape, occasional liberties were taken in the service of conveying her meaning and music.

Else was a performer—she wore flamboyant costumes with striking jewelry and masks. She often dressed as *Prince Jussuf of Thebes,* and accompanied her verses with flute, harmonica and bells. The music of her poetry is key. Fortunately her rhythm can usually be captured, as can her melodic tone, for many vowels and consonants are the same or similar in English, German's etymological cousin. The greatest obstacle in translating Lasker-Schüler's poetry into English is her simple song-like rhyme. Unless one is an Auden, combining end-rhyme with the original rhythm and correct meaning in a contemporary, natural and convincing English, that is beautiful and poetic, is difficult, if not impossible. Generally, I relied on half and internal rhymes, alliteration and accent, as well as other subtle musical elements to echo the sound of her poems.

Around 1980, two American translations of Lasker-Schüler's poetry appeared, embodying two different approaches. The first was *Hebrew Ballads and Other Poems,* translated by Audri Durchslag and Jeanette Litman-Demeestère, and published by the Jewish Publication Society. This selection of sixty poems emphasized Lasker-Schüler's role as a cultural icon of her time, focusing on her portrait poems, poems of historical and religious interest. In this enjoyable rendition the transla-tors satisfied themselves with reproducing as much of the poet's music as possible without forcing her rhymes. The second collection was *Your Diamond Dreams Cut Open My Arteries*, translated by Robert Newton and published by the University of North Carolina Press. The book's accurate, but unfortunately unpoetic title gives a foretaste of what can happen when a translator is totally faithful and literal in his translations. Newton's comprehensive collection of 145 poems, translated and rhymed to boot, is nevertheless an heroic attempt to make Lasker-Schüler's work more available to English-speaking readers.

In contrast, my own shorter selection of forty-three poems attempts to offer the essential core—the heart—of Else Lasker-Schüler's lyric legacy. Though these versions inevitably represent an interaction and melding of the talents and souls of both author and translator, I sincerely hope that they speak truthfully on behalf of their maker, transmitting somehow the moods, the light and shadow of her soul. Before her death, Else enigmatically confessed that her poems had not been written in German at all, but rather in Hebrew. At other times she said they were written in *Mystic Asiatic*. In that mysterious language of hers comes a poetry shimmering with the magic and wonder of a child, singing the sorrow and joy of our universal human journey. Today Lasker-Schüler is esteemed as prophet of a Jerusalem, a Thebes, a Tibet not of history but of the eternal spirit. "The maker of poetry," she explained in *The Land of the Hebrews*, "sinks to the depths of the world, and at the same time rises up to Heaven."

—*Janine Canan*

ELSE LASKER-SCHÜLER

GESAMTAUSGABE IN ZEHN BÄNDEN

VERLEGT
BEI PAUL CASSIRER
IN BERLIN

INTRODUCTION

"THE BLACK SWAN OF ISRAEL, a Sappho whose world has split in two...." So a friend of the poet, Else Lasker-Schüler, described her in her youth.

She came from the Rhineland, from a family of prosperous bankers, from an atmosphere in which Jewish religiosity and Western European culture formed a unity. Her father, Aron Schüler, was a man of humor and vitality, her mother, born Jeanetta Kopp, was beautiful, somewhat melancholy, an admirer of Goethe, said to have been something of a poet in her own right. Born February 11, 1869, Elisabeth was the youngest of six children, and enjoyed a measure of affection and security which she vainly sought in later years; her special temperament, in which playfulness and passionate religious feeling were inseparable, was evident from the first. As the child of Jewish parents she was subjected to minor persecutions on the part of classmates, but she never fell into the opposite religious prejudice; her older brother Paul, to whom she was very close, intended to convert to Catholicism but died before baptism at the age of twenty-one. It was the first of many losses that marked her path. Her mother died in 1890. In 1893 or 1894 she married a physician, Berthold Lasker, and went to live in Berlin, where she set up a studio as a painter. Even after she had settled on poetry as her chief vocation she continued to illustrate her poems with childlike yet powerful drawings. In 1897 her father died; in 1899 her son Paul was born. Her first marriage ended in 1900 or 1901; her first book of poems, *Styx,* appeared in 1902; it was dedicated to the memory of her parents.

She became a bird of paradise in the cafe society, the "Bohemian" literary world of Berlin. It was a paradox, the contrast between the rootless existence she was destined to lead and her continuing devotion to family and to the religion of her fathers, but it bespoke no inner inconsistency. She did not recognize the world of politicians and bureaucrats, the heartless everyday. And so she cut her hair short, dressed in Oriental costume, called herself Prince Jussuf of Thebes, or Malik, or Tino of Baghdad. Her second marriage—announced in 1903, but solemnized somewhat earlier—was to the writer and composer Georg Levin, whom she renamed Herwarth Walden. To her friends also she gave names: "Giselheer the Barbarian" is Gottfried Benn, the "Blue Rider" is Franz Marc; Georg Trakl and the painter Franz Marc were both influenced by her vision. It was a fated generation; Trakl and Marc died in the war, her friend Johannes Haltzmann—Senna Hoy, or Prince Sasha—was executed for revolutionary activities.

In 1912 her second marriage ended, and in the same year her favorite sister Anna died. From that year on she never had her own apartment, but lived in hotels and pensions. She was impulsive, generous, and unable to keep track of money, so that she had frequently to depend on the generosity of friends in turn. And she suffered bitterly from the commercial status of literature; her polemic against the publishing industry in "Ich räume auf"—"I Make a Clean Sweep"—is a "revolutionary" tirade based not on current political theory but on the feeling of the poet and the Jew for the sacredness of the word. The last of the great blows in her personal life came in 1927, when her son Paul, who had grown into a promising young painter, died at the age of twenty-eight.

Else Lasker-Schüler was among the first to see the coming threat to the Jewish nation; and when in 1933 she was struck down with an iron bar in the streets of Berlin, she reacted with an animal's instinct for survival: dazed, she went immediately to the railway station and entrained for Zurich, where she arrived penniless. There were no friends of hers in town; the Swiss literary public organized benefits for her after she had been arrested for vagrancy. By writing and painting she managed then to eke out a living in Zurich. From there she made three journeys to Jerusalem, in 1934, 1936, and 1939. The third time,

Kaarl Schmidt Rottluff

she intended to return again to Zurich; but she became ill on the journey, and she was deeply exhausted. And so she remained to the end of her life in the city whose fantastic image had been the goal of her childhood prayers. Here, too, she continued her literary activities, she became a familiar and exotic figure, she evoked affection and concern. But her last years were marked by grief for her family and for her people, a last hopeless passion, and the struggles of a temperament that rebelled furiously against old age. To the end she dressed as Prince Jussuf. It is said that in the last days of her life she went to a rabbi and asked him, "Listen, there are just the two of us here, do you believe in God?" She died in January, 1945, and was buried on the Mount of Olives.

Through all the vicissitudes the tone and style of Else Lasker-Schüler's poetry remained remarkably consistent. The note of lament for Israel never sounded more poignantly than in "My People," written in 1906; in force of passion "I Love You" from *My Blue Piano* is not surpassed by the earlier lyrics. Perhaps in the title poem of this last collection she attained the uttermost refinement of her music—thin, cold, ghostly, one seems to hear the stars clinking against each other like the chimes of a windharp—and yet it is the voice of a child. In reading her one is drawn into her world, which is both intimate and strangely static. The colors have the stillness of apparitions. In the love-poems the beloved is not so much described as invoked and adorned; as in the *Song of Songs* the feeling arises of a great beauty beyond sight. The rhythm of most of these poems is a surging and falling-back before the contemplated images—not an imitation of the melodies of the *Psalms* and the *Song of Songs*, but their legitimate continuation. A unique place in her work is held by the *Hebrew Ballads*, whose playfulness leaves in the end an uncanny impression. The figures are in motion and yet the motion seems also to have stopped; the rhythms lock into place like pieces of a mosaic. To the "Ballads" one can relate the astonishing "An Old Tibetan Carpet," in which the spatial and temporal mesh to a moving and breathing design.

One would be hard put to find in her work a line that does not bear her stamp, the seal and signature of a unique being. Many of the poems are not closed off, we feel them as utterances in that flow of speech which is the garment of an individuality. But on that garment there glisten a few perfect crystals of poetry—poems like "An Old Tibetan Carpet," "My Blue Piano," "A Love Song"—which are among the purest things ever written. These exist in three dimensions, though the names for those dimensions will probably remain forever secret.

The achievement of such individuality in creation—perhaps it is only possible in the work of one for whom a certain kind of abstraction does not exist, in the perspective of a religiosity which is both ancient and as fresh as a child's picture book. Her Judaism is really the religion of hearts and legends. She dreamed of a reconciliation between Judaism and Christianity—her poem on the Virgin is really another Hebrew Ballad—but the Christian concept of mediation is as foreign to her as the rationale of bureaucracy. Those whom she loves are her gods; and as for God, He was a close, if invisible relative: "If He knew a remedy," she said to someone in her last years, "surely He would tell it to *me.*" But she herself once wrote, "I have brought love into the world that every heart may bloom with a blue flower."

In Janine Canan the poems have found an ideal translator, a poet in whose own lines a kindred melody rises and falls. Perhaps these songs can enchant us too. Perhaps even here, today, Thebes is not so very far away.

—*Beatrice Cameron*

I

Song of the Blessed

(1884-1911)

DAS LIED DES GESALBTEN

Zebaoth spricht aus dem Abend:
Verschwenden sollst Du mit Liebe!
Denn ich will Dir Perlen meiner Krone schenken,
In goldträufelnden Honig Dein Blut verwandeln
Und Deine Lippen mit den Düften süßer Mandeln tränken.

Verschwenden sollst Du mit Liebe!
Und mit schmelzendem Jubel meine Feste umgolden
Und die Schwermut, die über Jerusalem trübt,
Mit singenden Blütendolden umkeimen.

Ein prangender Garten wird Dein Herz sein,
Darin die Dichter träumen.
O, ein hängender Garten wird Dein Herz sein,
Aller Sonnen Aufgangheimat sein,
Und die Sterne kommen, ihren Flüsterschein
Deinen Nächten sagen.
Ja, tausend greifende Aeste werden Deine Arme tragen,
Und meinem Paradiesheimweh wiegende Troste sein!

SONG OF THE BLESSED

Sabaoth speaks out of the evening:
Be prodigal—spend all your love!
So I may give you my crown pearls,
transform your blood into dripping gold honey,
and soak your lips in sweet almond scent.

Be prodigal—spend all your love!
And gild my feasts with molten jubilation,
planting in the melancholy that weighs on Jerusalem
singing umbrella blossoms.

And your heart will become a splendid garden
where poets dream.
Oh, your heart will become a hanging garden,
the homeland of every dawn,
and stars will enter your nights
whispering their light.
Yes, your arms will raise a thousand reaching branches,
and rocking will solace my passion to return to paradise!

SULAMITH

O, ich lernte an Deinem süssen Munde
Zu viel der Seligkeiten kennen!
Schon fühl' ich die Lippen Gabriels
Auf meinem Herzen brennen....
Und die Nachtwolke trinkt
Meinen tiefen Zederntraum.
O, wie Dein Leben mir winkt!
Und ich vergehe
Mit blühendem Herzeleid
Und verwehe im Weltraum,
In Zeit,
In Ewigkeit,
Und meine Seele verglüht in den Abendfarben
Jerusalems.

SHULAMITE

Oh, on your sweet mouth I came to know
too much of bliss!
Already I feel Gabriel's lips
blazing on my heart,
and the night cloud drinks
my deep cedar dream.
Oh, how your life beckons me!
And I perish
in flowering sorrow,
blowing away into space,
into time,
into eternity.
And my soul smoulders in the evening hues
of Jerusalem.

DIE LIEBE

Es rauscht durch unseren Schlaf
Ein feines Wehen, Seide,
Wie pochendes Erblühen
über uns beide.

Und ich werde heimwärts
Von deinem Atem getragen,
Durch verzauberte Märchen,
Durch verschüttete Sagen.

Und mein Dornenlächeln spielt
Mit deinen urtiefen Zügen,
Und es kommen die Erden
Sich an uns zu schmiegen.

Es rauscht durch unseren Schlaf
Ein feines Wehen, Seide—
Der weltalte Traum
Segnet uns beide.

LOVE

Through our sleep
a fine breeze rustles its silk—
like buds throbbing open
above us both.

And I am carried homeward
on your breath
through enchanted fairytales
and buried sagas.

My thorny smile plays
with your primal features
and earths come
to nestle beside us.

Through our sleep
a fine breeze rustles its silk—
the age-old dream
blessing us both.

DER ABEND RUHT AUF MEINER STIRNE

Der Abend ruht auf meiner Stirne,
Ich habe dich nicht murmeln gehört, Mensch,
Dein Herz nicht rauschen gehört—
Und ist dein Herz nicht die tiefste Muschel der Erde!
O, wie ich träumte nach diesem Erdton.
Ich lauschte dem Klingen deiner Freude,
An deinem Zagen lehnte ich und horchte,
Aber tot ist dein Herz und erdvergessen.
O, wie sann ich nach diesem Erdton...
Der Abend drückt ihn kühl auf meine Stirne.

THE EVENING RESTS ON MY BROW

The evening rests on my brow.
Man, I still haven't heard you murmur
or heard your heart roar—
and yet is not your heart
Earth's deepest shell?
How I dreamed that Earth tone.
Listening for the ring of your joy,
I leaned next to your fear and listened closely.
But your heart is dead and Earth forgotten.
Oh, how I imagined that tone—
the evening presses it coolly to my brow.

HEIMLICH ZUR NACHT

Ich habe dich gewählt
Unter allen Sternen.

Und bin wach—eine lauschende Blume
Im summenden Laub.

Unsere Lippen wollen Honig bereiten,
Unsere schimmernden Nächte sind aufgeblüht.

An dem seligen Glanz deines Leibes
Zündet mein Herz seine Himmel an—

Alle meine Träume hängen an deinem Golde,
Ich habe dich gewählt unter allen Sternen.

NIGHT SECRET

I have chosen you
among all these stars.

Am awake, a listening flower
in the buzzing bush.

Our lips long to make honey,
our shimmering nights are in full bloom.

From your body's holy spark
my heart lights its heavens.

All my dreams hang from your gold.
I have chosen you among all these stars.

WENN DU KOMMST

Wollen wir den Tag im Kelch der Nacht verstecken,
Denn wir sehnen uns nach Nacht.
Goldene Sterne sind unsere Leiber,
Die wollen sich küssen—küssen.

Spürst du den Duft der schlummernden Rosen
Über die dunklen Rasen—
So soll unsere Nacht sein.
Küssen wollen sich unsere goldenen Leiber.

Immer sinke ich in Nacht zur Nacht.
Alle Himmel blühen dicht von funkelnder Liebe.
Küssen wollen sich unsere Leiber, küssen—küssen.

WHEN YOU COME

Shall we hide day in the chalice of night,
since we long for the night.
Our bodies are golden stars
that want to kiss and kiss.

Do you smell the slumbering roses
upon the dark grass?
So will our night be—
our golden bodies long to kiss.

From night to night I keep falling—
heaven flowers thick with sparkling love.
Our golden bodies long to kiss—kiss and kiss.

EIN ALTER TIBETTEPPICH

Deine Seele, die die meine liebet,
Ist verwirkt mit ihr im Teppichtibet.

Strahl in Strahl, verliebte Farben,
Sterne, die sich himmellang umwarben.

Unsere Füße ruhen auf der Kostbarkeit,
Maschentausendabertausendweit.

Süßer Lamasohn auf Moschuspflanzenthron,
Wie lange küßt dein Mund den meinen wohl
Und Wang die Wange buntgeknüpfte Zeiten schon.

AN OLD TIBETAN CARPET

Your soul in love with mine
is woven with it in the Tibetan carpet.

Beam in beam, enamored colors,
stars that wooed across the heavens.

Our feet rest upon the treasure
thousands upon thousands of meshes wide.

Sweet lama son on a musk-plant throne,
how long has your mouth kissed mine.
And cheek upon cheek, how many lifetimes brightly tied.

ICH BIN TRAURIG

Deine Küsse dunkeln, auf meinem Mund.
Du hast mich nicht mehr lieb.

Und wie du kamst—!
Blau vor Paradies;

Um deinen süßesten Brunnen
Gaukelte mein Herz.

Nun will ich es schminken,
Wie die Freudenmädchen
Die welke Rose ihrer Lende röten.

Unsere Augen sind halb geschlossen,
Wie sterbende Himmel—

Alt ist der Mond geworden.
Die Nacht wird nicht mehr wach.

Du erinnerst dich meiner kaum.
Wo soll ich mit meinem Herzen hin?

I AM SAD

Your kisses darken on my mouth—
you no longer love me.

But how you once came—
blue for paradise.

On your ecstatic fountain
my heart danced.

Now I must paint it,
like the ladies who redden
the withered rose of their loins.

Our half-closed eyes
are like dying heavens.

The moon grows ancient.
And the night no longer watches.

You barely remember me—
where then shall I take my heart?

HEIMWEH

Ich kann die Sprache
Dieses kühlen Landes nicht,
Und seinen Schritt nicht gehn.

Auch die Wolken, die vorbeiziehn,
Weiß ich nicht zu deuten.

Die Nacht ist eine Stiefkönigin.

Immer muß ich an die Pharaonenwälder denken.
Und küsse die Bilder meiner Sterne.

Meine Lippen leuchten schon
Und sprechen Fernes,

Und bin ein buntes Bilderbuch
Auf deinem Schoß.

Aber dein Antlitz spinnt
Einen Schleier aus Weinen.

Meinen schillernden Vögeln
Sind die Korallen ausgestochen,

An den Hecken der Gärten
Versteinern sich ihre weichen Nester.

Wer salbt meine toten Paläste—
Sie trugen die Kronen meiner Väter,
Ihre Gebete versanken im heiligen Fluß.

HOMESICK

I cannot speak the language
of this cool country,
or keep its pace.

Even the fleeting clouds
I cannot interpret.

The night is a step-queen.

Forever I must remember Pharaoh's forests,
and kiss the image of my stars.

My lips sparkle brightly
and tell of faraway.

I am a colorful picture-book
lying open on your lap.

But your face spins
a veil of tears.

Out of my glittering birds
the corals have been gouged.

Upon the garden bushes
their soft nests turned to stone.

Who will consecrate my dead palaces?
They held the crowns of my ancestors,
whose prayers drowned in the holy stream.

MARIE VON NAZARETH

Träume, säume, Marienmädchen—
überall löscht der Rosenwind
Die schwarzen Sterne aus.
Wiege im Arme dein Seelchen.

Alle Kinder kommen auf Lämmern
Zottehotte geritten,
Gottlingchen sehen—

Und die vielen Schimmerblumen
An den Hecken—
Und den großen Himmel da
Im kurzen Blaukleide!

MARY OF NAZARETH

Dream and dally, maiden Mary—
the wind full of roses is blowing
out all the black stars.
Rock the sweet soul in your arms.

All the children come riding
giddy-up on lambs
to see darling God,

and the many flowers sparkling
on the bushes,
and the big sky—there
in the short blue dress!

II

Hebrew Ballads

(1905-1920)

VERSÖHNUNG

Es wird ein großer Stern in meinen Schoß fallen...
Wir wollen wachen die Nacht,

In den Sprachen beten,
Die wie Harfen eingeschnitten sind.

Wir wollen uns versöhnen die Nacht—
So viel Gott strömt über.

Kinder sind unsere Herzen,
Die möchten ruhen müdesüß.

Und unsere Lippen wollen sich küssen,
Was zagst du?

Grenzt nicht mein Herz an deins—
Immer färbt dein Blut meine Wangen rot.

Wir wollen uns versöhnen die Nacht,
Wenn wir uns herzen, sterben wir nicht.

Es wird ein großer Stern in meinen Schoß fallen.

ATONEMENT

A great star will fall in my lap—
let us keep watch all night,

pray in the tongues
which are carved like harps.

Let us make peace with the night—
so much God overflows.

Our hearts are children
who wish to rest sweetly weary.

And our lips long to kiss—
why do you hesitate?

Doesn't my heart verge upon yours.
Your blood turns my cheeks red.

Let us make peace tonight—
heart to heart, we shall not die.

A great star will fall in my lap.

MEIN VOLK

Der Fels wird morsch,
Dem ich entspringe
Und meine Gotteslieder singe...
Jäh stürz ich vom Weg
Und riesele ganz in mir
Fernab, allein über Klagegestein
Dem Meer zu.

Hab mich so abgeströmt
Von meines Blutes
Mostvergorenheit.
Und immer, immer noch der Widerhall
In mir,
Wenn schauerlich gen Ost
Das morsche Felsgebein,
Mein Volk,
Zu Gott schreit.

MY PEOPLE

The rock is crumbling
from which I arise
and sing my songs of God....
Suddenly I plunge from the path
and deep within stream
over wailing-stone
alone to the sea.

I have washed so far
from the ferment of my blood.
And still, within me, echoes the sound
when—shuddering eastward—
the crumbling rock-bones
of my People
cry out to God.

ABEL

Kains Augen sind nicht gottwohlgefällig,
Abels Angesicht ist ein goldener Garten,
Abels Augen sind Nachtigallen.

Immer singt Abel so hell
Zu den Saiten seiner Seele,
Aber durch Kains Leib führen die Gräben der Stadt.

Und er wird seinen Bruder erschlagen—
Abel, Abel dein Blut färbt den Himmel tief.

Wo ist Kain, da ich ihn stürmen will:
Hast du die Süßvögel erschlagen
In deines Bruders Angesicht?!!

ABEL

Cain's eyes are not pleasing to God.
Abel's face is a golden garden.
Abel's eyes are nightingales.

Abel always sings so clearly
to the strings of his soul.
But through Cain's body wind the city sewers.

And he will slay his brother—
Abel, Abel, your blood stains heaven darkly.

Where is Cain, when I mean to take him by storm?
Did you murder the sweet birds
in your brother's face!

HAGAR UND ISMAEL

Mit Muscheln spielten Abrahams kleine Söhne
Und ließen schwimmen die Perlmutterkähne;
Dann lehnte Isaak bang sich an den Ismael

Und traurig sangen die zwei schwarzen Schwäne
Um ihre bunte Welt ganz dunkle Töne,
Und die verstoßne Hagar raubte ihren Sohn sich schnell.

Vergoß in seine kleine ihre große Träne,
Und ihre Herzen rauschten wie der heilige Quell,
Und übereilten noch die Straußenhähne.

Die Sonne aber brannte auf die Wüste grell
Und Hagar und ihr Knäblein sanken in das gelbe Fell
Und bissen in den heißen Sand die weißen Negerzähne.

HAGAR AND ISHMAEL

Abraham's sons played with shells,
floating mother-of-pearl canoes.
Then frightened Isaac leaned on Ishmael.

Sadly the two black swans sang
ebony tones round their colorful world.
And banished Hagar grabbed her son,

shed in his small tear her great one.
Hearts rushing like the holy spring,
they sped past the ostrich cocks.

But the sun burned harshly on the desert.
Hagar and her boy sank in the yellow pelt,
dug their teeth in the sizzling sand.

JAKOB

Jakob war der Büffel seiner Herde.
Wenn er stampfte mit den Hufen,
Sprühte unter ihm die Erde.

Brüllend liess er die gescheckten Brüder.
Rannte in den Urwald an die Flüsse,
Stillte dort das Blut der Affenbisse.

Durch die müden Schmerzen in den Knöcheln
Sank er vor dem Himmel fiebernd nieder,
Und sein Ochsgesicht erschuf das Lächeln.

JACOB

Jacob was the bull of his herd.
When he pounded his hooves,
the Earth sparked under him.

Bellowing, he left his spotted brothers
and ran to the primal forest rivers
to soothe his bleeding monkey bites.

Ankles tired and aching,
feverish he sank before Heaven,
and his oxen face gave birth to the Smile.

PHARAO UND JOSEPH

Pharao verstösst seine blühenden Weiber,
Die duften nach den Gärten Amons.

Sein Königskopf ruht auf meiner Schulter,
Die strömt Korngeruch aus.

Pharao ist von Gold.
Seine Augen gehen und kommen
Wie schillernde Nilwellen.

Sein Herz aber liegt in meinem Blut;
Zehn Wölfe gingen an meine Tränke.

Immer denkt Pharao
An meine Brüder,
Die mich in die Grube warfen.

Saülen werden im Schlaf seine Arme
Und drohen!

Aber sein träumerisch Herz
Rauscht auf meinem Grund.

Darum dichten meine Lippen
Grosse Süssigkeiten,
Im Weizen unseres Morgens.

PHARAOH AND JOSEPH

Pharaoh casts off his blossoming wives—
they smell of Amon's gardens.

His kingly head rests on my shoulder,
that emanates the scent of corn.

Pharaoh is made of gold.
His eyes come and go
like iridescent Nile waves.

But his heart lies in my blood—
ten wolves ran to my wells.

Pharaoh ruminates
about my brothers,
who threw me into the pit.

In sleep his arms become pillars—
threatening!

But his dreamy heart
thunders in my depths.

Therefore my lips compose
vast sweetnesses
in the wheat of our dawn.

DAVID UND JONATHAN

O Jonathan, ich blasse hin in deinem Schoß,
Mein Herz fällt feierlich in dunklen Falten;
In meiner Schläfe pflege du den Mond,
Des Sternes Gold sollst du erhalten.
Du bist mein Himmel mein, du Liebgenoß.

Ich hab so säumerisch die kühle Welt
Fern immer nur im Bach geschaut…
Doch nun, da sie aus meinem Auge fällt,
Von deiner Liebe aufgetaut…
O Jonathan, nimm du die königliche Träne,
Sie schimmert weich und reich wie eine Braut.

O Jonathan, du Blut der süßen Feige,
Duftendes Gehang an meinem Zweige,
Du Ring in meiner Lippe Haut.

DAVID AND JONATHAN

Oh Jonathan, I faint away in your lap.
Solemnly my heart falls in dark folds.
Tend the moon in my temples carefully,
and you will be given the star's gold.
You are my heaven, my dear companion.

I have always hesitated, watching from afar
the cool world reflected in the stream.
Now it drops from my eye,
thawed by your love—
Oh Jonathan, take this royal tear,
shining soft and opulent as a bride.

Oh Jonathan, blood of the sweet fig
hanging fragrant from my branch—
you ring, piercing my lip.

ESTHER

Esther ist schlank wie die Feldpalme,
Nach ihren Lippen duften die Weizenhalme
Und die Feiertage, die in Juda fallen.

Nachts ruht ihr Herz auf einem Psalme,
Die Götzen lauschen in den Hallen.

Der König lächelt ihrem Nahen entgegen—
Denn überall blickt Gott auf Esther.

Die jungen Juden dichten Lieder an die Schwester,
Die sie in Säulen ihres Vorraums prägen.

ESTHER

Esther is slender as the field palm.
The wheat stalks and festivals of Judah
smell sweet like her lips.

At night her heart rests on a psalm.
Idols eavesdrop in the corridors.

The King smiles at her approaching step—
for everywhere God shines upon Esther.

Young Jews compose songs to their sister,
and carve them in pillars by her doorway.

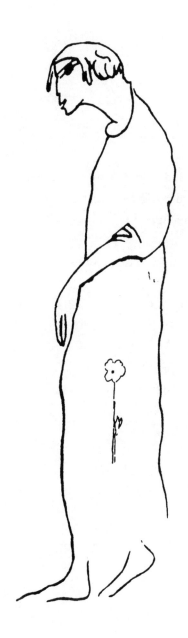

ZEBAOTH

Gott, ich liebe dich in deinem Rosenkleide,
Wenn du aus den Gärten trittst, Zebaoth.
O, du Gottjüngling,
Du Dichter,
Ich trinke einsam von deinen Düften.

Meine erste Blüte Blut sehnte sich nach dir,
So komme doch
Du süßer Gott,
Du Gespiele Gott,
Deines Tores Gold schmilzt an meiner Sehnsucht.

SABAOTH

God, I love you in your gown of roses,
as you step from the garden, Sabaoth.
Oh, my young God,
my Poet—
lonely, I drink from your fragrance.

The first bloom of my blood craved you,
so come,
my sweet God,
my playmate God,
your golden gate melts in my longing.

AN GOTT

Du wehrst den guten und den bösen Sternen nicht;
All ihre Launen strömen.
In meiner Stirne schmerzt die Furche,
Die tiefe Krone mit dem düsteren Licht.

Und meine Welt ist still—
Du wehrtest meiner Laune nicht.
Gott, wo bist du?

Ich möchte nah an deinem Herzen lauschen,
Mit deiner fernsten Nähe mich vertauschen,
Wenn goldverklärt in deinem Reich
Aus tausendseligem Licht
Alle die guten und die bösen Brunnen rauschen.

TO GOD

You restrain neither the good, nor the evil stars;
all their moods stream forth.
In my brow the furrow aches,
this deep crown of dusky light.

And my world is silent—
You have not restrained my mood.
God, where are You?

I'd like to lean upon your heart and listen,
immerse myself in your vast presence,
when gold-transfigured in your Realm
of infinitely blissful Light
all the good and the evil fountains roar.

III

Our Love Song

(1913–1923)

DEM BARBAREN

Ich liege in den Nächten
Auf deinem Angesicht.

Auf deines Leibes Steppe
Pflanze ich Zedern und Mandelbäume.

Ich wühle in deiner Brust unermüdlich
Nach den goldenen Freuden Pharaos.

Aber deine Lippen sind schwer,
Meine Wunder erlösen sie nicht.

Hebe doch deine Schneehimmel
Von meiner Seele—

Deine diamantnen Träume
Schneiden meine Adern auf.

Ich bin Joseph und trage einen süßen Gürtel
Um meine bunte Haut.

Dich beglückt das erschrockene Rauschen
Meiner Muscheln.

Aber dein Herz läßt keine Meere mehr ein.
O du!

TO THE BARBARIAN

At night I lie
upon your countenance.

On the steppes of your body
I plant almond trees and cedars.

Tirelessly I dig in your chest
for Pharaoh's golden joys.

But your lips are heavy—
my wonders do not release them.

Oh, raise your snowy heavens
off my soul!

Your diamond dreams
slice to my veins.

I am Joseph, wearing only a sweet sash
around my brightly colored skin.

The startled roar of my shells
makes you happy.

But your heart no longer lets the ocean in.
Oh, you!

ABER DEINE BRAUEN SIND UNWETTER...

In der Nacht schweb ich ruhlos am Himmel
Und werde nicht dunkel vom Schlaf.

Um mein Herz schwirren Träume
Und wollen Süßigkeit.

Ich habe lauter Zacken an den Randen,
Nur du trinkst Gold unversehrt.

Ich bin ein Stern
In der blauen Wolke deines Angesichts.

Wenn mein Glanz in deinem Auge spielt,
Sind wir eine Welt.

Und würden entschlummern verzückt—
Aber deine Brauen sind Unwetter.

BUT YOUR EYEBROWS ARE STORMS

At night I hover restlessly in the sky,
undarkened by sleep.

Around my heart dreams buzz,
searching for sweetness.

But my edges are spiked—
only you drink gold unharmed.

I am a star
in the blue cloud of your face.

When my rays shine in your eyes
we are one world.

And would fall blissfully asleep—
but your eyebrows are storms.

EIN LIEBESLIED

Aus goldenem Odem
Erschufen uns Himmel.
O, wie wir uns lieben...

Vögel werden Knospen an den Ästen,
Und Rosen flattern auf.

Immer suche ich nach deinen Lippen
Hinter tausend Küssen.

Eine Nacht aus Gold,
Sterne aus Nacht...
Niemand sieht uns.

Kommt das Licht mit dem Grün,
Schlummern wir;
Nur unsere Schultern spielen noch wie Falter.

A LOVE SONG

Out of golden breath
Heaven shaped us.
Oh, how we love one another.

Birds become buds on the branches,
and roses flutter away.

I search for your lips
behind a thousand kisses.

A night made of gold,
stars made of night—
no one can see us.

When day brings in the green,
we're slumbering—
only our shoulders still play like butterflies.

ABSCHIED

Ich wollte dir immerzu
Viele Liebesworte sagen,

Nun suchst du ruhlos
Nach verlorenen Wundern.

Aber wenn meine Spieluhren spielen
Feiern wir Hochzeit.

O, deine süßen Augen
Sind meine Lieblingsblumen.

Und dein Herz ist mein Himmelreich...
Laß mich hineinschaun.

Du bist ganz aus glitzernder Minze
Und so weich versonnen.

Ich wollte dir immerzu
Viele Liebesworte sagen,

Warum tat ich das nicht?

PARTED

I always longed to say to you
many words of love—

now you search restlessly
for lost wonders.

But when my music-clocks play,
we celebrate our wedding.

Oh, your sweet eyes
are my favorite flowers.

And your heart is my heavenly kingdom—
let me look inside.

You are pure glistening mint—
you daydream so tenderly.

I always longed to say to you
so many words of love—

why didn't I?

UNSER LIEBESLIED

Unter der Wehmut der Esche
Lächeln die Augen meiner Freundin.

Und ich muß weinen
Überall wo Rosen aufblühn.

Wir hören beide unseren Namen nicht—
Immer Nachtwandlerinnen zwischen den bunten Jünglingen.

Meine Freundin gaukelt mit dem Mond,
Unserm Sternenspiel folgen Erschrockene nach.

O, unsere Schwärmerei berauscht
Die Straßen und Plätze der Stadt.

Alle Träume lauschen gebannt hinter den Hecken
Kann nicht Morgen werden—

Und die seidige Nacht uns beiden
Tausendmalimmer um den Hals geschlungen.

Wie ich mich drehen muß!

Und meine Freundin küßt taumelnd den Rosigtau
Unter dem Düster des Trauerbaums.

OUR LOVE SONG

Out of the ash tree's sorrow,
my friend's eyes are smiling.

And I must cry
wherever roses bloom.

Neither of us can hear her name—
night-wanderers among the bright boys.

My friend juggles the moon.
The timid follow our game with the stars.

Oh, how our rapture enchants
the city streets and squares.

All the dreams listen spellbound behind the hedges.
Tomorrow never comes—

silken night wrapped round our necks
a-thousand-times-always.

How I must whirl!

And my friend, reeling, kisses the rosy dew
under mourning's dark tree.

ABSCHIED

Aber du kamst nie mit dem Abend—
Ich saß im Sternenmantel.

...Wenn es an mein Haus pochte,
War es mein eigenes Herz.

Das hängt nun an jedem Türpfosten,
Auch an deiner Tür;

Zwischen Farren verlöschende Feuerrose
Im Braun der Guirlande.

Ich färbte dir den Himmel brombeer
Mit meinem Herzblut.

Aber du kamst nie mit dem Abend—
...Ich stand in goldenen Schuhen.

FAREWELL

But you never came with the evening—
I sat in a cape of stars.

When I heard someone knocking,
it was my own heart.

Now it hangs on every door post,
even yours—

among ferns a burnt-out fire-rose
in garland brown.

For you I stained heaven blackberry
with my own heart's blood.

But you never came with the evening—
I stood in golden shoes.

EIN LIED

Hinter meinen Augen stehen Wasser,
Die muß ich alle weinen.

Immer möcht ich auffliegen,
Mit den Zugvögeln fort;

Buntatmen mit den Winden
In der großen Luft.

O ich bin so traurig——
Das Gesicht im Mond weiß es.

Drum ist viel samtne Andacht
Und nahender Frühmorgen um mich.

Als an deinem steinernen Herzen
Meine Flügel brachen,

Fielen die Amseln wie Trauerrosen
Hoch vom blauen Gebüsch.

Alles verhaltene Gezwitscher
Will wieder jubeln,

Und ich möchte auffliegen
Mit den Zugvögeln fort.

A SONG

Behind my eyes are waters—
I must weep them all.

I always long to fly away
with the migrating birds,

breathe colorfully with the winds
in the vast air.

Oh, I am so sad—
the Man in the Moon knows.

That's why so much velvety devotion
and early dawn surrounds me.

When my wings broke
against your stony heart,

blackbirds fell like funeral roses
down from the blue bushes.

All the chirping held back,
wants to rejoice again,

and I long to fly faraway
with the migrating birds.

MEINE MUTTER

War sie der große Engel,
Der neben mir ging?

Oder liegt meine Mutter begraben
Unter dem Himmel von Rauch—
Nie blüht es blau über ihrem Tode.

Wenn meine Augen doch hell schienen
Und ihr Licht brächten.

Wäre mein Lächeln nicht versunken im Antlitz,
Ich würde es über ihr Grab hängen.

Aber ich weiß einen Stern,
Auf dem immer Tag ist;
Den will ich über ihre Erde tragen.

Ich werde jetzt immer ganz allein sein
Wie der goße Engel,
Der neben mir ging.

MY MOTHER

Was she the great Angel
who walked beside me?

Or does my mother lie buried
under this sky of smoke—
it never blossoms blue over her death.

If only my eyes shone brightly,
bringing her light.

If my smile hadn't already sunk in my face,
I would hang it over her grave.

But I know a star,
where it is always day—
I want to place it over her world.

Now I shall always be alone
like the great Angel
who walked beside me.

DER ALTE TEMPEL IN PRAG

Tausend Jahre zählt der Tempel schon in Prag;
Staubfällig und ergraut ist längst sein Ruhetag
Und die alten Väter schlossen seine Gitter.

Ihre Söhne ziehen nun in die Schlacht.
Der zerborstene Synagogenstern erwacht,
Und er segnet seine jungen Judenritter.

Wie ein Glücksstern über Böhmens Judenstadt,
Ganz aus Gold, wie nur der Himmel Sterne hat.
Hinter seinem Glanze beten wieder Mütter.

THE OLD TEMPLE IN PRAGUE

The temple in Prague has stood for a thousand years.
Its sabbath long ago turned dusty and gray—
the ancient fathers closed its iron gate.

Now their sons go off to war.
A shattered synagogue star keeps watch
and blesses its young Jewish riders.

A lucky star over Bohemia's Jewish city,
pure gold as only the stars in Heaven.
Behind its rays, once again mothers pray.

MEIN STILLES LIED

Mein Herz ist eine traurige Zeit,
Die tonlos tickt.

Meine Mutter hatte goldene Flügel,
Die keine Welt fanden.

Horcht, mich sucht meine Mutter,
Lichte sind ihre Finger und ihre Füsse wandernde Träume.

Und süsse Wetter mit blauen Wehen
Wärmen meine Schlummer

Immer in den Nächten,
Deren Tage meiner Mutter Krone tragen.

Und ich trinke aus dem Monde stillen Wein,
Wenn die Nacht einsam kommt.

Meine Lieder trugen des Sommers Bläue
Und kehrten düster heim.

—Ihr verhöhntet meine Lippe
Und redet mit ihr.—

MY SILENT SONG

My heart is a sad time,
soundlessly ticking.

My mother had golden wings
that found no world.

Listen, my mother looks for me.
Her fingers are lights, her feet wandering dreams.

Sweet atmosphere with blue drifts
always warms my sleep—

in the nights
whose days wear my mother's crown.

And I drink silent wine out of the moon,
when night comes lonely.

My songs wore summer-blue
and returned home dusky.

You scorned my lips,
yet you speak with them!

Doch ich griff nach euren Händen,
Denn meine Liebe ist ein Kind und wollte spielen.

Und ich artete mich nach euch,
Weil ich mich nach dem Menschen sehnte.

Arm bin ich geworden
An eurer bettelnden Wohltat.

Und das Meer wird es wehklagen
Gott.

Ich bin der Hieroglyph,
Der unter der Schöpfung steht

Und mein Auge
Ist der Gipfel der Zeit;

Sein Leuchten küsst Gottes Saum.

And still I reached for your hands,
for my love is a child and wanted to play.

And I adapted to you,
because I longed for what is human.

I have become poor
from your begging charity.

And the ocean will lament it
unto God.

I am the hieroglyph
written beneath Creation.

And my eye
is the pinnacle of time.

Its light kisses God's hem.

GEBET

Ich suche allerlanden eine Stadt,
Die einen Engel vor der Pforte hat.
Ich trage seinen großen Flügel
Gebrochen schwer am Schulterblatt
Und in der Stirne seinen Stern als Siegel.

Und wandle immer in die Nacht...
Ich habe Liebe in die Welt gebracht—
Daß blau zu blühen jedes Herz vermag,
Und hab ein Leben müde mich gewacht,
In Gott gehüllt den dunklen Atemschlag.

O Gott, schließ um mich deinen Mantel fest;
Ich weiß, ich bin im Kugelglas der Rest,
Und wenn der letzte Mensch die Welt vergießt,
Du mich nicht wieder aus der Allmacht läßt
Und sich ein neuer Erdball um mich schließt.

PRAYER

In every country I seek a city
with an angel standing at the gate.
I carry broken on my shoulder
his great heavy wing,
and in my forehead the seal of his star.

And endlessly I roam the night
bringing love to this world,
that every heart may blossom blue.
All my wearying life I have watched,
darkly breathing, cloaked in God.

Oh God, pull your coat tighter!
I know I'm the lees in the goblet,
and when the last man pours out the world
You'll not let me slip through your might again—
a new globe of earth will encompass me.

IV

My Blue Piano

(1932-1945)

MEIN BLAUES KLAVIER

Ich habe zu Hause ein blaues Klavier
Und kenne doch keine Note.

Es steht im Dunkel der Kellertür,
Seitdem die Welt verrohte.

Es spielen Sternenhände vier
—Die Mondfrau sang im Boote—
Nun tanzen die Ratten im Geklirr.

Zerbrochen ist die Klaviatür.....
Ich beweine die blaue Tote.

Ach liebe Engel öffnet mir
—Ich aß vom bitteren Brote—
Mir lebend schon die Himmelstür—
Auch wider dem Verbote.

MY BLUE PIANO

At home I have a blue piano,
but cannot play a single note.

It stands in the dark of the cellar door,
ever since the world went savage.

Four starry hands play,
the Moon Lady sang in her boat.
Now rats dance to a clatter.

Its keyboard is shattered—
I weep over the dead blue thing.

Ah dear Angel, I have eaten
such bitter bread—please open
for me while still alive—even
though forbidden—Heaven's door.

ICH WEISS

Ich weiß, daß ich bald sterben muß
Es leuchten doch alle Bäume
Nach langersehntem Julikuß—

Fahl werden meine Träume—
Nie dichtete ich einen trüberen Schluß
In den Büchern meiner Reime.

Eine Blume brichst du mir zum Gruß—
Ich liebte sie schon im Keime.
Doch ich weiß, daß ich bald sterben muß.

Mein Odem schwebt über Gottes Fluß—
Ich setze leise meinen Fuß
Auf den Pfad zum ewigen Heime.

I KNOW

I know, that soon I must die.
Yet all the trees are glowing
from July's long-awaited kiss.

My dreams are fading—never
have I written a duller ending
in all my books of rhyme.

To greet me, you pick a flower—
I loved already in the bud.
Yes I know, that soon I must die.

My breath hovers over God's river—
softly I set my foot
on the path to my eternal home.

HERBST

Ich plücke mir am Weg das letzte Tausendschön....
Es kam ein Engel mir mein Totenkleid zu nähen—
Denn ich muß andere Welten weiter tragen.

Das ewige Leben *dem*, der viel von Liebe weiß zu sagen.
Ein Mensch der *Liebe* kann nur auferstehen!
Haß schachtelt ein! wie hoch die Fackel auch mag schlagen.

Ich will dir viel viel Liebe sagen—
Wenn auch schon kühle Winde wehen,
In Wirbeln sich um Bäume drehen,
Um Herzen, die in ihren Wiegen lagen.

Mir ist auf Erden weh geschehen....
Der Mond gibt Antwort dir auf deine Fragen.
Er sah verhängt mich auch an Tagen,
Die zaghaft ich beging auf Zehen.

AUTUMN

On my way I pick the last lovely daisy.
An angel has come to stitch my shroud—
for I must carry on other worlds.

Eternal life to *him,* wise enough to talk abundantly of love—
only a being of *love* rises from the grave.
Hate imprisons, however high the torch blazes.

So much, so much love I want to tell you—
even when the cold winds blow,
whirling around trees,
and hearts that once lay in their cradles.

On earth I was sorely wounded—
the Moon will answer any questions you raise.
Through a veil he watched me,
tip-toeing through days of fear.

EIN LIEBESLIED

Komm zu mir in der Nacht—wir schlafen engverschlungen.
Müde bin ich sehr, vom Wachen einsam.
Ein fremder Vogel hat in dunkler Frühe schon gesungen,
Als noch mein Traum mit sich und mir gerungen.

Es öffnen Blumen sich vor allen Quellen
Und färben sich mit deiner Augen Immortellen....

Komm zu mir in der Nacht auf Siebensternenschuhen
Und Liebe eingehüllt spät in mein Zelt.
Es steigen Monde aus verstaubten Himmelstruhen.

Wir wollen wie zwei seltene Tiere liebesruhen
Im hohen Rohre hinter dieser Welt.

A LOVE SONG

Come to me in the night—we'll sleep closely twined.
I am so tired and lonely from watching.
A strange bird sang in the dark dawn,
as my dream still wrestled with itself and me.

Now flowers open beside every spring,
colored with your Everlasting eyes.

Come to me in the night on seven-star shoes
and clothed in love, come late to my tent.
Moons are rising from Heaven's dusty chests.

Like two rare animals, let us take love's rest
in the tall reeds behind this world.

ICH LIEBE DICH.....

Ich liebe dich
Und finde dich
Wenn auch der Tag ganz dunkel wird.

Mein Lebelang
Und immer noch
Bin suchend ich umhergeirrt.

Ich liebe dich!
Ich liebe dich!
Ich liebe dich!

Es öffnen deine Lippen sich.....
Die Welt ist taub,
Die Welt ist blind

Und auch die Wolke
Und das Laub—
—Nur wir, der goldene Staub
Aus dem wir zwei bereitet:
—Sind!

I LOVE YOU

I love you
and find you,
even though the day grows dark.

All my life
until now—
I have wandered searching.

I love you!
I love you!
I love you!

Your lips are opening....
The world is deaf,
the world is blind,

even the cloud
and the leaf.
Only we two—made
of golden dust—
are!

IN MEINEM SCHOSSE

In meinem Schoße
Schlafen die dunkelen Wolken—
Darum bin ich so traurig, du Holdester.

Ich muß deinen Namen rufen
Mit der Stimme des Paradiesvogels
Wenn sich meine Lippen bunt färben.

Es schlafen schon alle Bäume im Garten—
Auch der nimmermüde
Vor meinem Fenster—

Es rauscht der Flügel des Geiers
Und trägt mich durch die Lüfte
Bis über dein Haus.

Meine Arme legen sich um deine Hüften,
Mich zu spiegeln
In deines Leibes Verklärtheit.

Lösche mein Herz nicht aus—
Du den Weg findest—
Immerdar.

IN MY WOMB

In my womb
the dark clouds sleep—
that's why I am so sad, my Sweet.

I must cry your name
with the voice of the bird-of-paradise,
whenever my lips blush crimson.

All the trees in the garden
have already fallen asleep—
even the tireless one by my window.

The wing of the hawk rustles,
lifting me up through the winds
to your house.

My arms embrace your hips,
mirroring me
in your body's effulgent light.

Do not extinguish my heart—
and always
you will find your way.

DEM HOLDEN

Ich taumele über deines Leibes goldene Wiese,
Es glitzern auf dem Liebespfade hin die Demantkiese
Und auch zu meinem Schoße
Führen bunterlei Türkise.

Ich suchte ewig dich—es bluten meine Füße—
Ich löschte meinen Durst mit deines Lächelns Süße.
Und fürchte doch, daß sich das Tor
Des Traumes schließe.

Ich sende dir, eh ich ein Tropfen frühes Licht genieße,
In blauer Wolke eingehüllte Grüße
Und von der Lippe abgepflückte eben erst erblühte Küsse.
Bevor ich schwärmend in den Morgen fließe.

TO THE BELOVED

I reel over your body's golden meadow—
diamond pebbles sparkle all along Love's way,
and turquoises of every shade
lead even to my lap.

Forever I sought you—my feet still bleed.
On your sweet smile I quenched my thirst.
And still I fear that the dream
will close its gate.

I send you—before I drink a drop of early light—
greetings wrapped in blue clouds,
and plucked from my lips, freshly opened kisses.
Before flowing blissfully out to the dawn....

MICH FÜHRTE IN DIE WOLKE

Mich führte in die Wolke mein Geschick—
Wir teilten säumerisch ein erdentschwertes Glück.

Ich dachte viel an Julihimmel—
Du sahst das Blau in meinem Blick.

Und schwebten mit den Vögeln auf
Ein Silberrausch...
Bevor die Welt brach das Genick.

Und auch wir beide blieben nicht verschont
—Und träumen trübe unterm bleichen Rosenstrauch im Mond
Die Lande unter uns: verblichnes Mosaik.

MY FATE LED ME INTO THE CLOUDS

My fate led me into the clouds—
lingering, we shared an earth-free happiness.

I thought often of July heaven—
you saw the blue in my eye.

And we soared with the birds
on a silver high—
until the world broke its neck.

And not even we were spared—
sadly we dream under the pale rose-bush in the Moon,
the nations below us a bleached mosaic.

MEINE FREIHEIT

Meine Freiheit
Soll mir niemand rauben.

Sterb ich am Wegrand wo,
Liebe Mutter,

Kommst du und hebst mich
Auf deinem Flügel zum Himmel.

Ich weiß dich rührte
Mein einsam Wandeln

Der spielende Ticktack
Meines Kinderherzens.

MY FREEDOM

No one shall rob me
of my freedom.

If I die somewhere along the way,
you will come, dear Mother,

and lift me on your wing
to Heaven.

I know you were touched
by my lonely wandering,

the playful tick-tock
of my childlike heart.

ICH SCHLAFE IN DER NACHT

Ich schlafe in der Nacht an fremden Wänden
Und wache in der Frühe auf an fremder Wand.
Ich legte mein Geschick in harten Händen
Und reihe Tränen auf, so dunkle Perlen ich nie fand.

Ich habe einmal einen blauen Pfad gekannt
Doch weiß ich nicht mehr wo ich mich vor dieser Welt befand.
Und—meine Sehnsucht will nicht enden!...

Vom Himmel her sind beide wir verwandt
Und unsere Seelen schweben übers Heilige Land
In *einem* Sternenkleide leuchtend um die Lenden.

I SLEEP AT NIGHT

I sleep at night by strange walls,
and wake at dawn by a strange wall.
I placed my fate in hard hands,
and now string tears—pearls so dark I never found.

Once I knew a path of blue.
But now cannot remember where I was, before this world.
And my nostalgia will not end!

You and I are both descended from Heaven.
And our souls float over the Holy Land
wearing *one* starry robe, brightly shining round the hips.

EIN EINZIGER MENSCH

Ein einziger Mensch is oft ein ganzes Volk
Doch jeder eine Welt
Mit einem Himmelreich wenn
Er der Eigenschaften uredelste pflegt:
Gott
Gott aufspriessen lässt in sich
Gott will night begossen sein
Mit Blut.
Wer seinen Nächsten tötet
Tötet im Herzen aufkeimend Gott
Wir können night mehr schlafen in den Nächten
Wir bangen mit den

A SINGLE HUMAN BEING (Unfinished)

A single human being is often a whole people,
yet each a world
with a Heaven when
he cultivates the oldest and noblest of qualities:
God—
lets God spring up within.
God does not want to be watered
with blood.
He who kills his neighbor,
kills God budding in his heart.
We can no longer sleep at night,
we are afraid.....

MEIN HERZ RUHT MÜDE

Mein Herz ruht müde
Auf dem Samt der Nacht
Und Sterne legen sich auf meine Augenlide....

Ich fließe Silbertöne der Etüde—
Und bin nicht mehr und doch vertausendfacht.
Und breite über unsere Erde: Friede.

Ich habe meines Lebens Schlußakkord vollbracht—
Bin still verschieden—wie es Gott in mir erdacht:
Ein Psalm erlösender—damit die Welt ihn übe.

EXHAUSTED, MY HEART RESTS

Exhausted, my heart rests
on the night's velvet,
and stars lie down on my eyelids.

I flow in the silver tones of an *étude*.
Am no more, and yet am multiplied a thousand times—
spreading over our Earth: Peace.

I completed my life's final chord—
quietly fading away—as God intended:
A saving psalm—meant for the world to practice.

Atonement

Franz Marc

JANINE CANAN is the author of eight poetry collections, including *Her Magnificent Body, Changing Woman* and *Love, Enter.* She edited the award-winning anthology *She Rises Like the Sun: Invocations of the Goddess by Contemporary American Women Poets,* and more recently *The Rhyme of the Ag-ed Mariness: Last Poems of Lynn Lonidier.* Her work appears in dozens of anthologies. Dr. Canan, a psychiatrist, resides in Sonoma, California.